The Alphabet in

The Alphabet in the Park
Selected Poems of Adélia Prado

Translated and with an Introduction
by Ellen Watson

Wesleyan University Press

WESLEYAN UNIVERSITY PRESS
Published by University Press of New England,
Hanover, NH 03755

Wesleyan Poetry in Translation

Some of these translations previously appeared in: *The Amer-ican Poetry Review, Antaeus, The Colorado State Review, Field, The Massachusetts Review, Paris Review, Writ,* and in *Woman Who Has Sprouted Wings: Poems by Contemporary Latin Amer-ican Women Poets,* published by Latin American Literary Re-view Press, 1988; *The Renewal of the Vision: Voices of Latin American Women Poets, 1940–1980,* Spectacular Diseases Im-print, Cambridge, U.K., 1987. Fifteen also appeared in a bilingual chapbook, *The Headlong Heart,* published by Liv-ingston University Press, 1988.

The translator wishes to thank Rosana Denise Koerich, Cris-tina Lopez, and, very especially, Verônica Cavalcanti for gen-erous help in translating these poems; the National En-dowment for the Arts for a grant that gave time to work on this book and made possible a trip to Brazil to work with Adélia Prado, whose warmth and guidance is greatly appreciated; and Paul Jenkins for his support and his inspired editing.

Library of Congress Cataloging-in-Publication Data
Prado, Adélia.
   [Poems. English. Selections]
   The alphabet in the park : selected poems of Adélia Prado / translated and with an introduction by Ellen Watson. —1st ed
      p. cm.
   Translated from the Portuguese.
   ISBN 0-8195-2175-2   —   ISBN 0-8195-1177-3 (pbk.)
      1. Prado, Adélia—Translations. English.   I. Watson,
   Ellen, 1950–. II. Title.
PQ9698.26.R29A6   1990
869.1—dc20   89-38463
                                                      CIP

Contents

Introduction   vii

Baggage (1976)

Dysrhythmia   3
Successive Deaths   4
Vigil   5
With Poetic License   6
Before Names   7
Lesson   8
Guide   9
Head   10
Two Ways   11
Praise for a Color   12
Purple   13
Seductive Sadness Winks at Me   14
Window   15
Heart's Desire   16
The Girl with the Sensitive Nose   17
Seduction   18
At Customs   19
Easter   20
Love Song   21
Serenade   22

The Headlong Heart (1977)

Concerted Effort   25
Not Even One Line in December   27
Day   28
A Man Inhabited a House   29
Lineage   30
A Good Cause   31
A Fast One   33
Absence of Poetry   34
Blossoms   35

Young Girl in Bed   36
The Black Umbrella   38
Passion   39
Neighborhood   42
Murmur   43
Denouement   44

Land of the Holy Cross (1981)

The Alphabet in the Park   47
Trottoir   49
Pieces for a Stained-Glass Window   50
Land of the Holy Cross   51
Falsetto   53
Some Other Names for Poetry   55
Tyrants   56
Love in the Ether   57
Consecration   58
Legend with the Word Map   60
Professional Mourner   61
Mobiles   62

Introduction

"Compared to my heart's desire/ the sea is a drop."

Adélia Prado's poetry is a poetry of abundance. These poems overflow with the humble, grand, various stuff of daily life—necklaces, bicycles, fish; saints and prostitutes and presidents; innumerable chickens and musical instruments. There is a lot of the color yellow here, and almost as much mathematics. And, seemingly at every turn, there is food.

I first met Adélia Prado in 1985, in her kitchen in Divinópolis. Ever since stumbling on a seven-line poem by her in an obscure Brazilian literary magazine, I had been wanting to sit across a table from this woman and talk about my translating the rage and delight of her poetry into English. When, years later, I arrived on her doorstep, manuscript of translations in hand, and blurted that I was famished, she was visibly pleased—the only other North American she had met had refused to eat a thing—and sat me down to a huge meal of beans and rice with all the trimmings.

Appetite is crucial to Prado:

> Forty years old: I don't want a knife
> or even cheese—
> I want hunger.

This poet cooks, eats, chews memories, confesses to gluttony: "I nibble vegetables as if they were carnal encounters."

Sexual hunger is admitted as frankly as any other. We see a woman tempted by "the vibrations of the flesh," by "the precise configuration of lips," who listens "most closely to the voice that is impassioned," a "woman startled by sex,/ but delighted."

There is an abundance of dark things also. There are "drowning victims, chopping blocks,/ forged signatures." There is cancer. There are moments of quiet desperation:

> What thick rope, what a full pail,
> what a fat sheaf of bad things.
> What an incoherent life is mine,
> what dirty sand.

The appeal of these poems has to do with their wonderful specificity, their nakedness, and their desire to embrace everything in sight—as well as things invisible. Here is a "creature of the body" who experiences great spiritual craving, who believes that the spirit is almost as palpable.

After all, the divine is only accessible to us via the concrete stuff of human existence. "From inside geometry/ God looks at me and I am terrified." The very thought inspires fear and awe, but it is an intimate, face-to-face spiritual encounter Prado is after: The word made flesh. She craves

> something that neither dies nor withers,
> is neither tall nor distant,
> nor avoids meeting my hard, ravenous look.
> Unmoving beauty:
> the face of God, which will kill my hunger.

What is truly astonishing in all this abundance of appetites is that Prado seems to revel in turning them loose in the same poem. What some might see as contradictory impulses appear and reappear obsessively, overlap and intertwine. For Prado, this is not only a fact of life but also the first step to understanding what it's like to live both in our bodies and out of them. "It's the soul that's erotic," she declares in one poem, and in another: "I know, now, that my erotic fantasies/ were fantasies of heaven." Hunger inspires hunger for the reverse: "There's no way not to think about death, among so much deliciousness, and want to be eternal." If God possesses an "unspeakable seductive power," it is also true that "a voluptuous woman in her bed/ can praise God,/ even if she is nothing but voluptuous and happy."

On the other hand, if at times "Sex is frail,/ even the sex of men," so is belief, whose buoyancy does not cancel the unacceptability of mortality. Death is a "trick." At times Prado is "tempted to believe that some things,/ in fact, have no Easter." The "furious love" of God "Who is a big mother hen" is often hard to understand:

> He tucks us under His wing and warms us.
> But first He leaves us helpless in the rain,
> so we'll learn to trust in Him
> and not in ourselves.

One of Prado's great gifts is knowing that embracing life means embracing impossible contradictions. The fear of death is inseparable from the pleasure of simply living. Sometimes one poem, or one line, seems to take back what another has said—"what I say, I unsay." But she also says: "what I feel, I write." For her, writing is a way to stay sane: "Poetry will save me." A way to gather, kicking and screaming, all the diverse reactions she has to the wide worlds—this one and the next.

This is a poetry of joy and desperation. Disarmingly childlike questions ("Does Japan really exist?"), the curious wonder of maps, mirrors, and trellises live alongside suicides, goose bumps, and shards of glass. I was not the least bit surprised that Prado's toast, over the shot of *cachaça* that followed the beans and rice, was "All or nothing!"

Saint Francis in the State of General Mines

Adélia Prado was born and has spent all her life in Divinópolis, Minas Gerais, a landlocked state of rugged mountains, mines (hence the name), and baroque churches. Minas is also known for producing more writers and presidents than any other state in Brazil, though Prado says of herself: "I am a simple person, a common housewife, a practicing Catholic." Since Mineiros are famous for their cautious self-containment, her words should not be taken at face value. Behind modesty and simplicity is the courage of a woman contesting taboos and traditions, a woman who extracts from her daily life in a small town of the interior extraordinary poems in which the sensual and the mystical, the sacred and the profane, fuse with unusual vividness.

Prado comes from a family of laborers, full of big life and small expectations, whose men worked for the railroad or ran small groceries and whose women (her mother and grandmothers) died in childbirth. From the start, she was the dreamer of the family, often accused of being lazy and odd because she liked nothing better than to sit and stare off into space. "Of my entire family, I'm the only one who has seen the ocean," as she says in "Denouement," and, in "Lineage," "None of them ever thought of writing a book." The first in her extended family to go to college, she earned degrees in philosophy and religious education, and taught the latter in public schools until 1979. Now married and the mother of five grown children, she has in recent years worked as cultural liaison for the city of Divinópolis.

Prado's literary career began relatively late—and with a bang—when elder statesman of Brazilian poetry Carlos Drummond de Andrade announced in his Rio de Janeiro newspaper column that Saint Francis was dictating verses to a woman in Minas Gerais. Though she had started writing when very young, she showed no one her work, and began to consider it poetry only in her late thirties, when she completed the manuscript of her first collection, *Bagagem* (Baggage). Drummond's pronouncement brought publishers to her door, and in the years since then she has produced five books of poems and three of poetic prose, steadily gaining recognition and admiration. The theatrical production of her poems and poetic prose, *Dona Doida: Interlude* (somewhat like the one-woman show of Emily Dickinson's work, *The Belle of Amherst*), performed by the great Brazilian actress Fernanda Montenegro, was a sensation in 1987, playing to packed audiences in Rio for nine months before beginning a national tour the following year.

Prado remains out of the limelight for the most part, traveling infrequently and somewhat reluctantly to Rio and São Paulo for interviews and to autograph her books. Though she has been a member of Brazilian writers' delegations to Portugal and to Cuba, she has little interest in cultivating literary contacts and takes no part in academic life. Her friendships with other writers are more about friendship than writing.

Traditional poetic forms and metrics find their way into Prado's poetry in spirit only, transformed into free verse based on the music of the spoken word, particularly the melody and rhythm of the colloquial Portuguese spoken in Minas Gerais. Biblical strains, particularly from Psalms and the Song of Solomon, can frequently be heard, as well as the poetry of the Mass and other Catholic rituals. The interplay of these various levels of diction reflects and underlines the constant play between human and divine in the sensibility that fuels the poems.

Certainly Prado's work has been influenced by the great poets of Brazilian modernism—Manuel Bandeira, Oswald de Andrade, Jorge de Lima, Carlos Drummond de Andrade, among others—especially in ironic humor and linguistic inventiveness. Several poems (not included here) acknowledge and explore her complex literary relationship with Drummond, the fellow Mineiro whose enthusiastic response brought her work to the attention of the rest of Brazil. When Prado is asked to name writers who have mattered to her, the first is invariably Guimarães Rosa (another Mineiro), said by some to be Latin America's greatest novelist, whose spiritual and linguistic presence is strong in these poems.

Prado's work depends very little on literary predecessors, however, springing almost entirely from her experience of daily and spiritual things, and the resulting authenticity has stunned many critics. "I find these poems brutal, marvelous, and astonishing," writes Margarida Salomão, in the preface to *Bagagem*. "This is a work before which critical discourse shrinks back, ashamed of all the abstractions, labels and schematics at hand, leaving to the reader's fascination this territory in which exuberance and clarity are not yet separated." In another review, poet and critic Affonso Romano Sant-Anna suggests that "Adélia Prado's success is due to the irrational and provocative power of her poetry. . . . Her poems leap past the cerebral and insufferable poetry of the last twenty years."

That the leaps these poems take seem convincingly uncalculated does not mean we are in the presence of a naïf. As poet Ferreira Gullar insists, "Prado's poetry is simple but not simple. . . . The overall impression is of a spontaneity that hides complexity and mastery." Hers is an elusive mastery, more a gift than an act of will, which she has developed in private, and which is virtually impossible to imitate successfully. "Some writers invent a rhetorical sleight-of-hand, patent it, and think it constitutes style," continues Romano Sant-Anna. "I'm talking about something else: a way of knocking the feet out from under us, leaving us humble and foolish in the face of a truth revealed."

Drummond's pronouncement rings true: "Adélia is lyrical, biblical, existential; she makes poetry as naturally as nature makes weather."

Emotional Weather

One of the things I like most about Prado's work is that her poems resist explication as thoroughly as they resist labels. They are neither obviously experimental nor easily traceable to a particular poetic forebear. They are fervent without agreeing to be partisan. They make conflicting claims, they admit to being pulled in opposite directions, they change their many minds.

This is not to say that Prado ducks and feints like a politician or that she cultivates obliqueness. This poet is as far from being middle-of-the-road as she is from striking poses. She is not concerned about opinion polls or academic reviewers. She gives us her unsorted-out self and she talks straight, which is why these poems are shocking.

The construction of the poems themselves reflects Prado's trust in the heart as the route to both mind and spirit. Form is not played with or labored over but allowed to happen. Her sense of line depends almost entirely on the breath of a phrase. Long and short lines stand side by side breathing to the rhythm of thought and association. Similarly, there are no stanza breaks. The poet feels no need to cue us when she is making a leap, no need to underline or italicize or aggrandize the shifting ground within the poem.

This way of writing entails a very different sense of completion. It is impossible to tell from where a poem begins where it will go, or from where it goes where it will end. Why, then, do they not seem arbitrary? Because for Prado neither life nor poetry is a free-for-all. If the poems seem to have no readily identifiable organizing principles, they most definitely possess a recurring modus operandi, which might be described simply as a belief in the supremacy of extreme feeling. Each poem starts with a specific image or moment or question or declaration and proceeds by association or obsession, letting in everything that insists on being let in until something tips the balance and the strongest emotion wins.

Emotion is treated as an undeniable fact, in and of itself, rather than as a cause for self-evaluation or soul-searching. Feelings enter the poem with or without specific events to explain them; love, grief, wonder—these visit all of us. What the poems present, and what determines how they are presented, is the process of how one emotional event takes precedence over another, how life is made of interruptions and reversals, how healing occurs as unexpectedly as pain.

"Who am I to organize the flight of the poem?" was Prado's response to my question about her way of writing. She sees poetry as open territory, open arms that refuse nothing. Each poem, then, is allowed to live its individual and multiple life without setting out to prove a point, provide a final solution, or better the previous one. A poem about sex is likely to touch at least fleetingly on faith and loss and aging. The poem merely (merely!) tumbles out the way a newborn baby does, twisting and turning, perhaps, along the way, but spilling out whole.

Prado uses this image of the newborn to describe what she does with the poem once it has tumbled out. Revision, she says, takes the form of cleaning away the placenta and the cheese and the bloody evidence of the process of birth, until all that is left is the infant itself, to stun us with its separate self as well as its inborn relation to all who tumbled out before.

Selecting poems for this volume of translations was at times as difficult and heartrending as I imagine it would be to decide which of many perhaps not equally lovable but equally deserving children to adopt. For the most part, I tried to follow Prado's example, letting instinct be the guide, though there were instances where poems close to my heart had to be left out because they presented unusual obstacles in the precarious journey from Portuguese to English. All the poems included are from Prado's first three volumes of poetry; two more appeared, in 1987 and 1988.

My aim in these translations has been to re-create the energy and accessibility of Prado's voice, to make inviting, disconcerting poems in English that express the urgent rage and delight of the originals. Occasionally this has entailed bending or even changing an image; at times it has meant accepting the impossibility of finding a word or phrase in English that carries with it all the connotations of the corresponding phrase in Brazilian Portuguese, and, instead, trying to add those layers of meaning somewhere else in the poem.

During the time we spent together in 1985, Prado not only patiently answered my innumerable questions, but also was interested in understanding what this business of bringing her poems to another language involved. A few days after I arrived in Divinópolis, she brought out the *American Poetry Review* that contained thirteen of my translations—her first publication in English. As irrepressibly playful and dead serious as she is in her poems, she smiled and confessed that she understood not a word, and wondered if I would be willing to paraphrase them back into Portuguese without looking at the originals. In addition to some gasps of delight at what I had done, there was anger, or at least consternation, at places where I had opted to stray from the literal, from the image as she had conceived it.

Several days later, in the middle of reading a poem of mine in Portuguese translation alongside my paraphrase of the original, she burst out: "But this isn't what you intended at all here! He translated the metaphor literally, and it just doesn't work the same way in Portuguese!" At that point, our collaboration reached a new level.

Our two-week-long conversation about poetry skipped and wandered and catapulted all over—just as Prado's poems do—but we kept circling back to her belief that metaphor is the guardian of reality, that faith, dream, and emotion are as real, if not more real, than the teacup on the table between us. We talked about the translator as an actor "interpreting" a text for a larger audience than those who speak the author's idiom. Toward the end of my stay, I asked her what she thought was most important for me to keep in mind as I "acted out" her poems in English. Be faithful to the emotion that generated the original, she said. Don't be clever; let yourself get carried away; re-create feelings, not words.

I share with Adélia Prado the belief that truth resides in the body. The mind must have its say, but, first and last, follow the heart. I have tried in these translations to be true to the insatiable size of the author's desire.

ELLEN WATSON

 Baggage
1976

Dysrhythmia

Old people spit with absolutely no finesse
and bicycles bully traffic on the sidewalk.
The unknown poet waits for criticism
and reads his verses three times a day
like a monk with his book of hours.
The brush got old and no longer brushes.
Right now what's important
is to untangle the hair.
We give birth to life between our legs
and go on talking about it till the end,
few of us understanding:
it's the soul that's erotic.
If I want, I put on a Bach suite
so I can feel forgiving and calm.
What I understand of God is His wrath;
there's no other way to say it.
The ball thumping against the wall annoys me,
but the kids laugh, contented.
I've seen hundreds of afternoons like today.
No agony, just an anxious impatience:
something is going to happen.
Destiny doesn't exist.
It's God we need, and fast.

3

Successive Deaths

When my sister died, I cried a great deal
and was quickly consoled. There was a new dress
and a thicket in the back yard where I could exist.
When my mother died, I was consoled more slowly.
There was a newfound uneasiness:
my breasts were shaped like two hillocks
and I was quite naked.
I crossed my arms over them when I cried.
When my father died, I was never again consoled.
I hunted up old pictures, visited acquaintances,
relatives, who would remind me of how he talked,
his way of pursing his lips and of being certain.
I imitated the way his body curled
in his last sleep and repeated the words
he said when I touched his feet:
"Never mind, they're all right."
Who will console me?
My breasts fulfilled their promise
and the thicket where I exist
is the genuine burning bush of memory.

Vigil

Nocturnal terror lopped off my hand
just as I reached for my nightclothes.
I stopped in the middle of the room, a pool
of clearheadedness so vast,
all at once everything turned incomprehensible.
The shape of the bed, so square and expectant,
the saw handle sticking out of nowhere, my nakedness
in transit between door and chair.
Utterly legible and inscrutable: a cloudless meadow
of sun and air, the children's laughter in a field
shredded by a tractor, the silver wedding anniversary
of the man who is always saying: "What did I do wrong
that I feel like being dead?"
A family built its house upon the hill;
if I so much as move my foot it will coming tumbling down.
The Spirit of God, setting in motion what pleases Him,
moves the young lady (I swear she's not a poet)
to say, full of grace: "Wouldn't it be just too funny
to see the President suck an orange!"
The Spirit of God is merciful,
He's going to abandon me so I can rest,
He's going to let me sleep.

With Poetic License

When I was born, one of those svelte angels
who plays a trumpet proclaimed:
this one will carry a flag.
A heavy load for a woman,
even nowadays such a bashful species.
I accept the subterfuges that fit;
no need to lie.
I'm not so ugly that I can't get married,
I think Rio's a real knockout, and—
well, yes and no, I believe in childbirth without pain.
But what I feel, I write. I make good on the prophecies.
I establish lineages, whole kingdoms
(pain is not bitterness).
My sadness has no pedigree
but my longing for joy—
its root goes back a thousand generations.
It's man's curse to be lame in life,
woman's to unfold. I do.

Before Names

I don't care about the word, that commonplace.
What I want is the grand chaos that spins out syntax,
the obscure birthplace of "of," "otherwise,"
"nevertheless," and "how," all those inscrutable
crutches I walk on.
Who understands language understands God,
Whose Son is the Word. It kills you to understand.
Words only hide something deeper, deaf and dumb,
something invented to be silenced.
In moments of grace, rare as they are,
you'll be able to snatch it out: a live fish
in your bare hand.
Pure terror.

Lesson

It was a shadowy yard, walled high with stones.
The trees held early apples, dark
wine-colored skin, the perfected flavor of things
ripe before their time.
Clay jugs sat alongside the wall.
I ate apples and sipped the purest water,
knowing the outside world had stopped dead from heat.
Then my father appeared and tweaked my nose,
and he wasn't sick and hadn't died, either;
that's why he was laughing, blood
stirring in his face again,
he was hunting for ways to spend this happiness:
where's my chisel, my fishing pole,
what happened to my snuffbox, my coffee cup?
I always dream something's taking shape,
nothing is ever dead.
What seems to have died fertilizes.
What seems motionless waits.

Guide

Poetry will save me.
I feel uneasy saying this, since only Jesus
is Saviour, as a man inscribed
(of his own free will)
on the back of the souvenir crucifix he brought home
from a pilgrimage to Congonhas.
Nevertheless, I repeat: Poetry will save me.
It's through poetry that I understand the passion
He had for us, dying on the cross.
Poetry will save me, as the purple of flowers
spilling over the fence
absolves the girl her ugly body.
In poetry the Virgin and the saints approve
my apocryphal way of understanding words
by their reverse, my decoding the town crier's message
by means of his hands and eyes.
Poetry will save me. I won't tell this to the four winds,
because I'm frightened of experts, excommunication,
afraid of shocking the fainthearted. But not of God.
What is poetry, if not His face touched
by the brutality of things?

Head

Whenever I had an attack of nerves
I would refuse to walk under electric wires,
I was afraid of rain, of lightning,
and I got nauseous just thinking about certain animals
which I won't mention (or I'd have to wash out my mouth
                    with ashes).
I would pick up every fruit peel in sight.
Now that I'm cured, I have a life and so much more:
already I can touch the wires when the switch is off,
and I got myself this plastic rain cape
which I wear day and night, even when I'm sleeping.
If it happens to rain, no problem.
I don't bother any more about fruit peels, even banana or mango;
let somebody else take care of them;
the signs I put up all over—"BEWARE"—
work just fine. It's really quite charming
for a bishop to have apostolic zeal.
I never tire of explaining this to the pastor
of my diocese, but he doesn't understand,
he merely says: "Oh, dear. Dear, dear";
he thinks it's women's lib, he thinks
faith is way up there and here below
there's only bad taste. It's awful, just awful—
no one understands. I used to scream continuously
when I had an attack of nerves.

Two Ways

From inside geometry
God looks at me and I am terrified.
He makes the incubus descend on me.
I yell for Mama,
I hide behind the door
where Papa hangs his dirty shirt;
they give me sugar water to calm me,
I speak the words of prayers.
But there's another way:
if I sense He's peeking at me,
I think about brands of cigarettes,
I think about a man in a red cape going out
in the middle of the night to worship the Blessed Sacrament,
I think about hand-rolled tobacco, train whistles, a farm woman
with a basket of *pequi* fruit all aroma and yellow.
Before He knows it, there I am in His lap.
I pull on His white beard.
He throws me the ball of the world,
I throw it back.

Praise for a Color

Yellow infers from itself papayas and their pulp,
penetrable yellow.
At noon: bees, sweet stinger and honey.
Whole eggs and their nucleus, the ovum.
That interior thing, minuscule.
From the blackness of the blind viscera,
hot and yellow, the minuscule speck,
the luminous grain.
Yellow spreads and smooths, a downpour
of the pure light of its name,
tropicordial.
Yellow turns on, turns up the heat,
a charmed flute,
an oboe in Bach.
Yellow engenders.

Purple

Purple puts on the squeeze.
Purple is tart and narrow.
Tyrant purple goes straight for the heart,
crazy for dawn.
Jesus's passion is purple and white,
very close to joy.
Purple is tart; it will ripen.
Purple is handsome and I like him.
Yellow likes him.
The sky purples morning and evening,
a red rose growing older.
I gallop after purple,
a sad memory, a four o'clock flower.
I round up love to turn me purple with passion,
I who choose and am chosen.

Seductive Sadness Winks at Me

I'm looking for the saddest thing, which once found
will never be lost again, because it will follow me
more loyal than a dog, the ghost
of a dog, sadness beyond words.
I have three choices: the first, a man,
still alive, calls me to his bedside
and says in his softest voice: "Pray for me to sleep, will you?"
Or, I dream I'm beating a little boy. I beat him and beat him
until my arm is decomposing and he's black and blue. I beat him
                    some more
and he laughs, without anger, he laughs at me who beats him.
In the last (and I personally create this horror),
the siren shrieks, calling a man who's already dead, and keeps
shrieking through the night till dawn and he doesn't return
and the siren insists and her voice is human.
If that's not enough, try this:
I lift my son by his sensitive organs
and he kisses me on the face.

Window

A pretty word, window.
Window: the wingbeat of the yellow butterfly.
Two carelessly painted wooden shutters open out,
clumsy blue window.
I jump in and out of you, ride you like a horse,
my foot dragging the ground.
Window on the open world, from where I saw
Anita, expecting, get married, Pedro Cisterna's
mother urinating in the rain, from where I saw
my love arrive on a bicycle and say to my father:
I have only the best intentions regarding your daughter.
O wooden-latched window, child's play for thieves,
peephole on my soul,
I look into my heart.

Heart's Desire

I'm no matron, mother of warriors, Cornelia,
but a woman of the people, mother of children, Adélia.
I cook and I eat.
Sundays I bang the bone on the plate to call the dog
and toss out the scraps.
When it hurts, I yell ouch,
when it's good, I'm brutish,
impulses beyond control.
But I have my crying spells,
little clarities behind my humble stomach,
and a booming voice for hymn singing.
When I write the book bearing my name
and the name I will give it, I'll bring it to a church,
to a tombstone, to the wilderness,
to cry and cry and cry,
elegant and odd as a lady.

The Girl with the Sensitive Nose

Don't wanna eat, mom
(big enamel kettle on a corner of the stove)
don't wanna eat, mom
(rice and beans, thick macaroni)
don't wanna eat, mom
(no tomato sauce)
don't wanna eat, mom
(tastes like sawdust)
don't wanna eat, mom
(that smell of acetylene gas)
don't wanna eat
(saw a cat on the way home, teeming with fleas)
don't wanna eat, mom
(when we get electric lights and dad
gives up on the gas lantern, that's when I'll eat).
Let's leave it dark, mom. Use the kerosene lamp,
not the gas, please—the blue part smells,
it seeps into your skin, in the food, in your thoughts,
takes the shapes of things. It's like when you get mad, mom,
so mad you can't yell, that's how bad the gas is,
the blue part. I'm gonna throw up, mom. Don't wanna eat now.
I'll wait for the electricity.

Seduction

Poetry catches me with her toothed wheel
and forces me to listen, stock-still,
to her extravagant discourse.
Poetry embraces me behind the garden wall, she picks up
her skirt and lets me see, loving and loony.
Bad things happen, I tell her,
I, too, am a child of God,
allow me my despair.
Her answer is to draw her hot tongue
across my neck;
she says *rod* to calm me,
she says *stone, geometry,*
she gets careless and turns tender,
I take advantage and sneak off.
I run and she runs faster,
I yell and she yells louder,
seven demons stronger.
She catches me, making deep grooves
from tip to toe.
Poetry's toothed wheel is made of steel.

At Customs

All I could offer, unblemished, were
my tears in response to beauty or fatigue,
a tooth dangling roots,
my bias in favor of everything baroque
in music, and Rio de Janeiro,
which, when I visited once, took my breath away.
"Not good enough," they said. And demanded
the foreign language I hadn't learned,
the record of my misplaced diploma
in the Ministry of Education, plus a tax on vanity
in all its forms—obvious, unusual, or insidious,
and why not?—although their ways
of detecting vanity were unusual and insidious.
Every time I apologized they said:
"You're acting polite and humble out of pride,"
and piled on the duties, and the ship left
while we were wrangling.
Then, as I grabbed my tooth and my trip to Rio,
ready to weep with fatigue, came the last straw:
"The roots stay here, as security."
There went my tooth.
Now I have just three unblemished items for collateral.

Easter

Age
is a way of feeling cold that takes me by surprise
and a certain acidity.
The way a dog curls up
when the lights go out and people go to bed.
I divide my day into three parts:
the first to look at photographs,
the second to look in mirrors,
the third, and longest, to cry.
Once blonde and lyrical,
I am not picturesque.
I ask God
on behalf of my weakness,
to abbreviate my days and grant me the face
of an aging, tired mother, a good grandmama,
I don't care which. That's what I aspire to
in my impatience and pain.
Because there's always someone
smack dab in the middle of my happiness saying:
"Don't forget your overcoat."
"You wouldn't have the nerve!"
"Why aren't you wearing your glasses?"
Even a dried rosebud with its powdery perfume—
I want something sweet like that,
something which says: that's her.
So I won't be afraid of posing for a picture,
so I'll be handed a poem on parchment.

Love Song

First came cancer of the liver, then came the man
leaping from bed to floor and crawling around
on all fours, shouting: "Leave me alone, all of you,
just leave me be," such was his pain without remission.
Then came death and, in that zero hour, the shirt missing
                    a button.
I'll sew it on, I promise,
but wait, let me cry first.
"Ah," said Martha and Mary, "if You had been here,
our brother would not have died." "Wait," said Jesus,
"let me cry first."
So it's okay to cry? I can cry too?
If they asked me now about life's joy,
I would have only the memory of a tiny flower.
Or maybe more, I'm very sad today:
what I say, I unsay. But God's Word
is the truth. That's why this song has the name it has.

Serenade

Some night under a pale moon and geraniums
he would come with his incredible hands and mouth
to play the flute in the garden.
I am beginning to despair
and can see only two choices:
either go crazy or turn holy.
I, who reject and reprove
anything that's not natural as blood and veins,
discover that I cry daily,
my hair saddened, strand by strand,
my skin attacked by indecision.
When he comes, for it's clear that he's coming,
how will I go out onto the balcony without my youth?
He and the moon and the geraniums will be the same—
only women of all things grow old.
How will I open the window, unless I'm crazy?
How will I close it, unless I'm holy?

The Headlong Heart
1977

Concerted Effort

The flatiron was invented
because of Eternal Life.
Or else why bother to crease trousers
if every ending is worm-eaten wood,
bones so clean there's no need for nausea?
Which is also why
metaphysicians hatch soliloquies,
good governments govern with justice,
and I'm wearing a low-cut dress.
My desire for the handsome young man
lives on,
it's written on my fingernails,
and grows with their roots.
Can a woman have twenty orgasms?
I don't worry about such silly details.
I want love, superior love.
I can tolerate only seven sorrows.
One more, and I go numb, playing my guitar.
Cemeteries are holy ground, that's why they attract me
after I get over being repelled.
Even if people insist: Look, there where your father was—
a splinter of rotting wood,
ribbons of cloth and dust.
He's crossed over, I say,
this silence is a trick, sheer expectation,
it's exactly what hope is when it doesn't rattle.
I know all about the burial, the lapse, the autopsy,
I realize there are drowning victims, chopping blocks,
                    forged signatures.
But why do you think pendulums swing?
After the grave, the clock goes on ticking,
someone makes coffee, everybody drinks it.
The boy went blind, his mother went crazy the day after,
silly the second,

and by the third was on the front porch leafing through a
                fashion magazine
because she wants a cool dress
to scare off the heat.
I had intended to whine, to throw up my arms, tempted
to sin against the Holy Spirit.
But life won't let me. And what I say
ends up brimming with joy.

Not Even One Line in December

I never want to desire death
unless out of holiness,
calling it *sister*, as Saint Francis did.
Almost the twenty-fifth and not one line.
My hips moving back and forth
and me not trying to contain the wiggle—
I should have walked like this my whole life
if I wanted to conquer the world.
Dusky butterflies, trash, pebbles,
soapy water seeping from the wall,
things offer themselves up to me
as I roam the neighborhood.
A little girl watches from her tiled porch,
and not even a line.
My work is important because it's all I have.
In a three-bedroom house with a tired back yard
the soul keeps moaning *ah, life*. . . .
The idea of suicide appears
and floats past the TV antenna,
but it keeps coming back, and not even a line.
I need to confess to a man of God:
I committed gluttony, I craved
the details of other people's frailties,
and—even though I have a husband—
I explored my own body.
Not even one line in December, and I was born for this!
My soul longs to copulate!
The Wise Men rush past me, the star is in hiding,
it's raining torrents in Brazil.

Day

The chickens open their beaks in alarm
and stop, with that knack they have,
immobile—I was going to say immoral—
wattles and coxcombs stark red,
only the arteries quivering in their necks.
A woman startled by sex,
but delighted.

A Man Inhabited a House

Death's charm, its disastrous spell,
is due to life,
because heaven is to the west of my father's house
where reside all the riches of the world and my soul.
There's a corner of the room
where I go to eat secretly, plate in hand,
from whence I see Jerusalem, its sparkling domes,
the Rose of Jericho in bloom.
From that perspective,
grave diseases look tame,
my cousin and her five bastard children, innocent.
Gunshots, alcohol, carelessness, even fear
settle in a cup of tea and sink to the bottom
thick with compassion and sugar,
indefatigable patience.
The bruised medicinal herbs add an aroma to the holiness
of the struggle to repeat: Oh, God, yes,
yes, my body is weak,
yes, I miss my bicycle,
the way I would dash off into the street flaunting
my invincible dominion over gullies and stones,
yes, youth affects me this much,
yes, and my weariness which is nothing at all
compared to what You suffered for me, oh, Father, on the cross.
Does the body feel pain?
This is what I ate:
plain rice, beans, and raw onion,
but the plate had a painted border.
The spoon was tarnishing,
but there were forget-me-nots engraved on the handle.
The body experiences joy, the tongue eats it:
bright, hot, unquestionable as suns.
Do we die?
I understand mathematics better.

Lineage

My gynecological tree
passed down noble,
marbleized gestures:
my father, on his wedding day,
left my mother behind and went to a dance.
She had only one dress, but what bearing,
what legs! What silk stockings she deserved!
My paternal grandfather sold green tomatoes;
it didn't work out. He demolished whole jungles
for charcoal, pores black with ashes to the end of his life:
"Don't bury me in Jaguara, no, not in Jaguara."
My maternal grandfather had a small grocery,
a kidney stone, suffered excessively
from bellyaches and the cold,
and hoarded cheese and coins in his wooden strongbox.
None of them ever thought of writing a book.
Extreme sinners, one and all, penitent
until the public confession of sins,
which one proclaimed as if for all:
"All men go astray. It doesn't do any good
to say *not me*. All men go astray.
Anyone who hasn't is about to."
There's no way to improve this maxim,
it's so tied up with their tears
the moment they were shed,
and it remained, intact, until I—
whose mother and grandmothers died young,
in childbirth—without comment
passed it on to my heirs,
overwhelmed
by a pain so high,
so deep,
a pain so beautiful,
in the midst of green tomatoes and charcoal,
moldy cheese and bellyaches.

A Good Cause

The President is dying.
I cry, wanting my tears to be the most definitive of all,
and I cry for this very vanity.
Poets before me have cried, and better, and more beautifully,
and more deeply, and not just for the death of the king,
but for mine, yours, their own,
for the miserable condition of being human. Nevertheless,
the reasons to cry have not been exhausted.
My power is small, I govern a few memories:
a plate, a tablecloth, one Sunday,
the sweet smell of orange peel.
Good and Evil escape me, even though and because they
                    inhabit me.
Day escapes me, the hour, all the hours;
I write a poem and delude myself that I've escaped sadness.
I merely make it rhythmic, lighter perhaps.
I do my best to make it beautiful, bearable,
and for that reasonless reason I cry some more.
The President is dying: it's very sad.
Spring Lamb with Fava Beans—
who, at a time like this, can take heart from cookbooks?
Self-propelled sex droops, weighted down, wilted.
The moon is a planet, a guitar is wood and gut.
I take advantage of the fact that the President is dying
and cry for my tooth decay, my varicose veins,
the ugly skirt about to cross the street, the humble elbow,
the head full of bobby pins, looking regal.
I cry because I'm about to remake myself and laugh out loud
and ask incorrigibly after the phase of the moon
and sow flower seed and set out vegetables.
I cry because I've relapsed into pleasure like a little boy
and, old as I am, this is humiliating.
I cry for having browbeat myself on behalf of happiness,
such a proud heart, lacking naturalness.
The President is dying: it's a good cause.
I take advantage of it and cry for the Brazilian people,

for the Southern Cross, which only now I realize
might not belong to us.
The Land of Vera Cruz, Santa Cruz, the Land of the Holy Cross,
Caminha's letter home, a harbinger of our future:
"This country will go far, my Lord King."
The Land of Palm Trees in whose shadow I weep, incongruous.
By birth and taste, by destiny, and now by hard choice
I covet the song-thrush, the President alive, the fish alive,
my father alive and hoarse from yelling:
VIVA! VIVA! VIVA!
It's hard to die faced with life,
life so hard to understand,
impossible not to love.
Infinite life which in order to continue disappears
and takes another form and sprouts anew,
a tree once pruned now blossoming,
its root immersed in God. Oh, God,
my eyeball aches, cramped from crying,
my soul is sad; I'd like to quit my job.
No hot food for this houseful today.
I'm not bathing, or combing my hair, or seeing anyone,
a tiny retaliation against the pain of living.
Anything that can sadden will continue,
as well as anything laughable, delectable.
Life will go on, repetitive.
Life will go on being new.
Itself. Naked.
Anyone who has ever lived has said the word Cross,
the word Father, bowing his or her head
and saying, at least once, from the depths of weariness:
"Oh, dear God," and would have given a kingdom
for the simple dwelling place of joy.
Lord, console us, have pity.
"Victory shall come from Your hand,
from Your divine arm."

A Fast One

Love wants to hug you but can't.
The crowd crowds around
with its malicious eyes,
placing shards of glass on top of the wall
so that love will give up.
Love turns to the post office,
but the post office tricks him,
the letter doesn't arrive,
love doesn't know whether he is or isn't.
Love jumps on horseback,
hops off the train,
arrives at the door worn out
from so much walking.
He speaks the word lily,
asks for water, drinks coffee,
sleeps in your presence,
sucks on a mint.
All cleverness, artifice, ingenuity:
If you're not careful, love will catch you,
eat you up, drench you.
But water love's not.

Absence of Poetry

He who made me took me away from plenty;
forty days he's been tormenting me in the desert.
The politician died, poor guy.
He wanted to become president and didn't.
My father wanted to eat.
My mother wanted to wander.
I'm in favor of the revolution but first I want a rhythm.
Dear God, my son asks for my blessing—I give it.
I, who am bad.
Why not even wasp's honey for me?
I, who said in the town square (exposing myself),
"Let's dance, you ragamuffins, follow the beat,
the Kingdom is implicit but real"—
I don't know where to go with this:
"The steeples are most eternal at two in the afternoon."
I see the mango tree against the black cloud,
my heart warms,
once more I delude myself that I will make the poem.
Everything she learned on the street
the converted tart does for mystical ecstasy:
so what if the seamstress comes to the door
sucking her cavity?
I still think she's pretty.
Some things that tempt me: physical beauty,
the precise configuration of lips,
sex, the telephone, letters,
the bitter shape of the mouth of *Ecce Homo*.
Dear God of Bilac, Abraham and Jacob,
will this cruel hour not pass?
Pluck me from this sand, oh, Spirit,
redeem these words from dust.
In this tropical country a hard winter rages.
I'm wearing socks, a jacket and distress.

Blossoms

The moonflower spread its wide blossoms,
each one a white skirt.
If I played the piano, they'd dance.
They make the world seem so good
I'm not even ashamed of wanting a husband.
They perfume the night.
The pipe of a little boy who never died
pipes on, wandering and sweet.
I go about my parish duties cheerfully
and never tire of waiting:
any day now, something wonderful might happen—
the five wounds, the flying saucer, the poet with his horse
whinnying at my door.
I wanted Mama and Papa's blessing, I wanted so much
to collect some birdcalls, some corners of the afternoon,
the balance of all that balances on the wind,
and play it on the flute. It's so good
I don't even care about God not letting me
be beautiful and young
(one of my soul's desires).
"The spirit of God hovered above the waters. . . ."
Above me hover these blossoms
and I am tougher than time.

Young Girl in Bed

Papa coughs, letting me know he's near,
and inspects the window latches one by one.
The roof beam is peroba wood,
I can sleep soundly. Mama tucks me in with a prayer
and I'm off, chasing after men,
trying not to be too greedy, letting good win out.
If I touch myself, I unleash the throngs,
shoals of little fish.
Mama knows all about the topaz burning in me,
that's why she says (a little enviously):
Get to sleep, it's late.
Yes, Mama, I'm on my way:
I'll stroll around the plaza with no one to scold me.
Bye-bye, I can take care of myself, I'll camp out
in the back alleys, befriended by boys from the bars
with guitars and eyes that won't leave me alone.
When the city is snoring in mist
the seminarians will be waiting for me in the sanctuary.
Heaven is right here, Mama!
It's a good thing I'm not a book
steeped in the catechism of Christian doctrine,
I can postpone my scruples and ride horseback
through the apathy of the well-pruned chrysanthemums.
Tomorrow I'll worry about the pretty wine stain
wilted flowers make on the ground.
Meanwhile, factories have their courtyards,
walls have nooks and crannies to hide behind.
They're nice to me in the barracks.
No, no tea, Mother dear,
it's Friar Crisóstomo's hand I want,

anointing me with holy oil.
I want passion from life.
And slaves, please—I'm weary.
With my love of crossness and theater,
I want my folding cot, I want
the holy angel of the Lord,
my zealous guardian.
But relax—he's a eunuch, Mama.

The Black Umbrella

Forgotten on the table,
handle upturned
and edges folded,
he's like his master, dressed
and laid out in the coffin.
Not extended at the joints,
not hung on that serious arm
which, since it was his master,
is underground by now.
As for him, he's bound for the cellar.
There's an ancient photo where he posed, open,
with the owner, a young man without spectacles.
Umbrella for rain, umbrella for sun,
umbrella for the piercing memory
of all that was a little ridiculous
and innocent in us.
Umbrella for life, black accordion file,
dog of mourning, sprawled dog.

Passion

Once in a while God takes poetry away from me.
I look at a stone, I see a stone.
The world, so full of departments,
is not a pretty ball flying free in space.
I feel ugly, gazing in mirrors to try to provoke them,
thrashing the brush through my hair,
susceptible to believing in omens.
I become a terrible Christian.
Every day at this time the sound of a giant mortar and pestle:
Here comes Gimpy, I think, and sadden with fear.
"What day is today?" says Mother;
"Friday is the day of sorrowful mysteries."
The night-light glimmers its already humble ray,
narrowing once and for all the black of night.
Enter, in the calm of the hour, the buzz
of the factory, in continuous staccato.
And I am in heat, unceasingly,
I persist in going to the garden to attract butterflies
and the memory of the dead.
I fall in love once a day,
I write horrible letters, full of spasms,
as if I had a piano and bags under my eyes,
as if my name were Anne of the Cross.
Except for the eyes in photographs,
no one knows what death is.
If there were no clover in the garden,
I don't know if I would write this;
no one knows what talent is.
I sit on the porch watching the street,
waiting for the sky to sadden with dusk.
When I grow up I'll write a book:
"You mean fireflies are the same thing as lightning bugs?" they
                    asked, amazed.
Over leftover coals, the beans

balloon in the black pot.
A little jolt: the end of the prayer long gone.
The young pullets did not all fit
under the mother hen;
she clucked a warning.
This story is threatening to end, stopped up with stones.
No one can stand to be merely Lenten.
A pain this purple induces fainting,
a pain this sad doesn't exist.
School cafeterias and radio broadcasts
featuring calisthenics set to music
sustain the order of the world, despite me.
Even the thick knots extracted from the breast,
the cobalt, its ray pointed at pained flesh—
upon which I have cast this curse:
I refuse to write one line to you—even these
settle in among the firewood,
longing for a place in the crucifixion.
I started this letter bursting with pride,
overestimating my ability to yell for help,
tempted to believe that some things,
in fact, have no Easter.
But sleep overpowered me and this story dozed off
letter by letter. Until the sun broke through.
The flies awoke.
And the woman next door had an attack of nerves;
they called to me urgently from the garden wall.
Death leaves behind photographs, articles of clothing,
half-full medicine bottles, disoriented insects
in the sea of flowers that covers the body.
This poem has gone sticky on me. He won't shake loose.
He disgusts me, with his big head;
I grab my shopping bag,

I'll stroll around the market.
But there he is, brandy in his spittle,
heels callused like a woman's,
coins in the palm of his hand.
It's not an exemplary life, this, robbing an old man
of the sweet pleasure of grandchildren.
My sadness was never mortal,
it's reborn every morning.
Death doesn't stop the pitter-pat of rain on the umbrella,
tiny droplets
innumerable as the constellations.
I trail behind the funeral procession,
mixing with holy women,
I wipe the Sacred Visage.
"All you who pass by, look and see
if there is any sorrow like my sorrow. . . ."
"What day is this?" asks Mother;
"Sunday is the day of glorious mysteries."
Happiness alone has body:
Head hung low,
glassy eyes and mouth,
bruised feelings and bruised limbs.

Neighborhood

The young man has finished his lunch
and is picking his teeth behind his hand.
The bird scratches in the cage, showering
him with canary seed and bird droppings.
I consider picking one's teeth unsightly;
he only went to primary school
and his bad grammar grates on me.
But he's got a man's rump so seductive
I fall desperately in love with him.
Young men like him
like to wolf their food:
beef and rice, a slice of tomato
and off to the movies
with that face of invincible weakness
for capital sins.
I feel so intimate, simple,
so touchable—because of love,
a slow samba,
because of the fact that we're going to die
and a refrigerator is a wonderful thing,
and the crucifix his mother gave him,

its gold chain against that frail chest . . .
He scrapes at his teeth with the toothpick,
he scrapes at my strumpet heart.

Murmur

Sometimes I get up at daybreak, thirsty,
flecks of dream stuck to my nightclothes,
and go look at the children in their beds.
Right then what I'm most sure of is: we die.
It bothers me not to have coined the wonderful phrase
at cock's crow. The children go on snoring.
Fragments, in sharp focus: his hands
crossed on his chest like the dead,
that little cut on his shoulder.
The girl today so intent on a new dress
is now fast asleep, oblivious,
and this is terribly sad
after she told me: "I think it would be even better
with a ruffle!" and cracked a half-smile,
embarrassed by so much happiness.
How is it that we mortals get bright-eyed
because a dress is blue and has a bow?
I take a sip and the water is bitter,
and I think: Sex is frail,
even the sex of men.

Denouement

I have great admiration for ships
and for certain people's handwriting which I attempt to imitate.
Of my entire family, I'm the only one who has seen the ocean.
I describe it over and over; they say "hmm"
and continue circling the chicken coop with wire.
I tell about the spume, and the wearisome size of the waters;
they don't remember there's such a place as Kenya,
they'd never guess I'm thinking of Tanzania.
Eagerly they show me the lot: this is where the kitchen will be,
that's where we'll put in a garden.
So what do I do with the coast?
It was a pretty afternoon the day I planted myself in the window,
                    between uncles,
and saw the man with his fly open,
the trellis angry with roses.
Hours and hours we talked unconsciously in Portuguese
as if it were the only language in the world.
Faith or no, I ask where are my people who are gone;
because I'm human, I zealously cover the pan of leftover sauce.
How could we know how to live a better life than this,
when even weeping it feels so good to be together?
Suffering belongs to no language.
I suffered and I suffer both in Minas Gerais and at the edge of the ocean.
I stand in awe of being alive. Oh, moon over the backlands,
oh, forests I don't need to see to get lost in,
oh, great cities and states of Brazil that I love as if I had invented them.
Being Brazilian places me in a way I find moving
and this, which without sinning I can call fate,
gives my desire a rest.
Taken all at once, it's far too intelligible; I can't take it.
Night! Make yourself useful and cover me with sleep.
Me and the thought of death just can't get used to each other.
I'll tremble with fear until the end.
And meanwhile everything is so small.
Compared to my heart's desire
the sea is a drop.

Land of the Holy Cross
1981

The Alphabet in the Park

I know how to write.
I write letters, shopping lists,
school compositions about the lovely walk
to Grandmother's farm which never existed
because she was poor as Job.
But I write inexplicable things too:
I want to be happy, that's yellow.
And I'm not, that's pain.
Get away from me sadness, stammering bell,
people saying between sobs:
"I can't take it any more."
I live on something called the terrestrial globe,
where we cry more
than the volume of waters called the sea,
which is where each river carries its batch of tears.
People go hungry here. Hate each other.
People are happy here, surrounded by miraculous inventions.
Imagine a certain Ferris wheel
whose ride makes you dizzy—
lights, music, lovers in ecstasy.
It's terrific! On one side the boys,
on the other the girls—me, crazy to get married
and sleep with my husband in our little bedroom
in an old house with a wood floor.
There's no way not to think about death,
among so much deliciousness, and want to be eternal.
I'm happy and I'm sad, half and half.
"You take everything too seriously," said Mother;
"go for a walk, enjoy yourself, take in a movie."
Mother doesn't realize that movies are like Grandfather said:
"Just people going by—if you've seen one,

you've seen them all."
Excuse the expression, but I want to fall in life.
I want to stay in the park, the singer's voice
sweetening the afternoon.
So I write: afternoon. Not the word,
the thing.

Trottoir

I know, now, that my erotic fantasies
were fantasies of heaven.
I thought sex lasted the whole night
and only at dawn did the bodies part.
The revelation that we are not angels
came to me rather late.
The king is in love—they say in a whisper—
I delight in imagining his voice,
his hand loosening the heavy crown from his forehead:
"Come, it's been so long since I've seen brown eyes;
I've been in the wars. . . ."
The unadorned king,
his sex erectible but contained,
tenacious as I am, squeezing from voice,
hands and eyes (virtually motionless) a wine,
a purple lushness, biting, semisweet,
the intoxication of a stroll among the stars.
I listen most closely to the voice that is impassioned,
to pulse beats, black holes in the chest,
instantaneous swoons,
where this pagan thing appears luminescent:
a black man making a meal of round-leafed
greenery at the edge of the precipice.
At the edge of sleep, at the edge of what I do not explain
a light shines. And with impetuous hope
the heel of my shoe on the curb
tappitytappitytaps.

Pieces for a Stained-Glass Window

Does Japan really exist?
Or any country I don't know, with its parched coastline?
What's between the thighs is public. Public and obvious.
What I want is your heart, the depths of your eyes
which do everything but speak.
If you look at me in Spanish, I'll snap my fingers
and start dancing, dressed in red.
When I closed my eyes to the sun, I saw a blueprint,
perfection, for only a second
and then forgot.
Just as the saints existed, so does God
with His unspeakable seductive power.
He's the one who made gold, and gave us the discretion
to invent necklaces to wear around our necks.
Said like that it's so pure I hardly see the sin
in buying one myself.
I've got the same desires as thirty years ago,
immutable as mosquitoes in the sun-drenched kitchen,
my mother making coffee
and my father seated, waiting.

Land of the Holy Cross

At my golden wedding anniversary, greedy as the grandchildren,
I'm going to eat sweets.
I will not look serene, like portraits
of women who ate and spoke little.
Because the monk killed himself
in the thicket outside the abbey.
It's been said before: There will be no consolation.
And there was: music, poetry, strolls.
Love has rhythms which are not those of sadness:
the shape of waves, impulse, running water.
Well, then—what do I say to the man, to the train,
to the little boy waiting for me,
to the myrtle tree blooming out of season?
Contemplating the impossible makes you crazy.
I'm a lowly tapeworm in God's intestine:
Well, then—well, then—well, then?
Where were the custodian, the steward, the gatekeeper?
Where was the rest of the brotherhood when you went out,
unlucky Brazilian boy, to meet that tree?
I am my own enemy. Torturers go crazy in the end,
eat excrement, hate their own obscene gestures;
unjust regimes fester.
While you were walking around in circles, divided soul,
what was she doing, saint and sinner, our Mother Church?
Promoting bingo, blessing new buildings, naturally,
but still: she produced you—no one dares deny it—
you and other saints who leave behind marked Bibles.
"We carry within us our own death sentence."
"Love your enemies."
He who said: "Whosoever believeth in Me
shall have everlasting life"—
He, too, swung from a piece of wood
like a fruit of scorn.
Nothing, nothing that is human is grand.
A little girl interrupts, pounding at the door,

asking for vine cuttings.
My hair stands on end.
Like a torturer I yank out the cutting,
the eyes, the entrails of the intruder,
and no better than Job I repent my nonsense.
There's always someone to ask Judas which tree is best:
lucid madmen, mad saints,
those to whom more was given, the almost sublime ones.
My biggest grandeur is to ask: Will there be consolation?
These would fit in a thimble:
my faith, my life, and my greatest fear
which is traveling by bus.
Temptation tests me and almost makes me happy.
It's good to ask help of our Lord God of the Army,
our God Who is a big mother hen.
He tucks us under His wing and warms us.
But first He leaves us helpless in the rain,
so we'll learn to trust in Him
and not in ourselves.

Falsetto

The authorities have bags under their eyes
and practiced voices for communiqués:
We guarantee the best solution on the spot.
Which spot? The pudendum?
God already took care of that, covering it with hair.
My son was a good boy.
He would never have killed himself like the police said.
I touched his head; it was all broken,
a token of their guilt.
The witnesses vanished,
lost their teeth, their tongues,
lost their memories.
I lost my son.
". . . He greeted the rabble, speaking to them of the Kingdom,
to those in need of cure he restored their health."
Hard words only for liars, legalists
who harness on others the heavy bundles
they themselves would not so much as touch . . .
Oh, great shriek that I long to shriek,
hiss that would leave me empty.
Certain hues, tamed birds,
a yellow house with a gate and flowers thrill me,
but I can't enjoy them. I've got to preach the Kingdom.
I'd like a country place, a wisp of a farm,
but Christianity won't let me,
Marxism won't let me.
Oh, great shriek in the face of palaces
churchly or otherwise:
DIVIDED WE FALL,
UNITED WE STAND!
My swimming pool is not for recreation, said the Pope.
I have no intention of being a prophet, said the Bishop.
What thick rope, what a full pail,
what a fat sheaf of bad things.
What an incoherent life is mine,

what dirty sand.
I am an old woman with whom God toys.
Along with rage and shame
my appetite remains unshakable—
fatty meats, anything floury,
I nibble vegetables as if they were carnal encounters,
I am afraid of death
and think about it at great length
as if I were a respectable, serious,
prudent and frugal lady-philosopher.
If someone will join me, I'll found a political party,
I'll overthrow the government, the papacy,
bulldoze all the rectories
and institute my dream:
across a plain, innumerable,
the friars descended in their hoods
like brown birds, peacefully, searching for a place.
I walked with them until they came to a big house.
Where they found a big stove, a big table,
and they all went inside and made themselves at home,
scattering about the house
like true brothers.

Some Other Names for Poetry

I'd like an abandoned city
so I could find things in the houses,
iron objects,
a fascinating picture on the wall
forgotten in the rush.
But without a visible war and with life so expensive,
who leaves behind so much as a needle?
The only place I find things
is in the rich cellar of dreams,
things I'll never possess.
All my life I've resisted Plato, with his broad shoulders,
his crippled Republic where poets are exiled.
After all, errors in translation are rife,
and I don't know Greek—
I never went through a sack of salt with him.
What he said or what I say
is meat thrown to the wild beasts—
but not what we dream.
There are no lies in dreams,
where everything is naked and we're unarmed.
Plato's myth—maybe he wrote it against his will;
who knows?—is as I tell it:
there's a hole in the corpse's throat
big as the valley of Jehoshaphat where we will be judged.
No power in the world picks a fight
when the subject is light and shadow,
the morning dew on a horse's mane or snout.
But the legions of darkness get furious
and the coroner's office (for suspicious reasons)
hides the photograph of the alleged suicide.
While love, which they don't believe in,
goes on impassive, spawning just sentences,
blessings, lovers—
in spite of the corpse
and its ruined neck.

Tyrants

Uncle Joaquim was an unabashed dictator.
Only one of the cousins dared to get married;
the others stayed home to honor his memory
with peevishness and small excitements.
They produced crochet and hilarity
(telling tales), virtue
and patience, which were squandered
on misplaced pride, irate Catholicism.
They spent their mutual bitterness on embroidery and greed:
the chicken coop is Alvina's, the flower bed
is Rosa's, the soda pop is Marta's—
but it's in Aurora's refrigerator.
They wouldn't set foot in church for their sister's wedding:
Aunt Zila is failing, soon
she'll be in Glory.
With no one to wait on, the cousins
will surely quarrel, grabbing
for rosaries, needles, doorknobs.
But if someone knocks, they'll serve up cookies
and the story about the tightrope-walking mouse
(which I always request):
"One day Papa was asleep on the sofa when he heard
a little noise: chin-chin, chin, chin-chin. . . ."
I'm touched by these cousins, aunts and uncles in frames on
                    the wall,
mice, in the middle of the pitched battle of that house,
looking to nibble the leftovers of what, after all, was love.

Love in the Ether

There's a landscape inside me
between noon and two P.M.
Long-legged birds, their beaks slicing the water,
enter and don't enter this memory-place,
a shallow lagoon with slender reeds along the shore.
I live there, when the desires of the body,
those metaphysicians, exclaim:
How lovely you are!
I want to excavate you until I find
where you keep so much feeling.
You think of me, and your secret half-smile
crosses sea and mountain,
gives me goose bumps,
love beyond the natural.
The body is as light as the soul,
minerals soar like butterflies.
All of it from this place
between noon and two P.M.

Consecration

Come! I will show you the bride. . . .
—Apocalypse 21:9

It was at home: Mama was cooking,
I was taking care of the baby.
Restless, because of the boy who was waiting for me.
The baby's wet, I called,
I'm going to change him.
Mama shot me a look and I went to my room
and tried on dresses to wear to the door
and talk with the boy who whispered:
I want to eat your legs, your belly, your breasts,
I want to touch you.
And he was in fact touching me, the way his soul
shone through his eyes.
Have you changed the baby?
You're a strange one!
Stop talking to your friends and listen!
I began to cry: pleasure and embarrassment.
He looked at my bare feet and laughed.
The vibrations of the flesh sing hymns,
even those we turn away from:
flatulence (he said in one ear)
yawns (he said in the other)
the rhythm of pleasure.
—I was worried the whole time.
—And so naïve and naked, he added,
a voluptuous woman in her bed
can praise God,
even if she is nothing but voluptuous and happy.
—Poor people understand that. . . .
—Yes, like when they write on the walls:
US BEGGARS SALUTE YOU, O GOD!
He looked like an angel, speaking of wisdom. . . .
Helios, I called him, you're that luminescent,

your body acting out your spirit.
—You learn fast, praise be Our Lord Jesus Christ,
he intoned from the bottom of his Christian soul,
enticing me once and for all.
Who is the pope? I asked, anxious to receive the sacraments.
—Our Father Who blesses us.
And he called me cow, as if he were saying flower, saint,
lucky prostitute.

Legend with the Word Map

Thebes, Midian, Mount Hor.
Sphinx-like names.
Idumea, Ephraim, Gilead.
Stories that don't demand my undivided attention.
Maps relax me,
the deserts more than the oceans
I don't dive into
because even on maps they're deep,
voracious, untamed.
How can we conceive of a map?
Here rivers, here mountains, ridges, gulfs,
or woodlands, as scary as the sea.
The legends of maps are so beautiful
they make travel superfluous.
You're crazy, they tell me, a map is a map.
I'm not, I reply.
A map is the certainty that *the place* exists;
maps contain blood and treasure.
God talks to us in the map in his geographic voice.

Professional Mourner

What a fate—that of the flowers
covering the woman in her coffin.
More difficult to understand than the thousand-sided polygon!
The tree duck sits on her eggs,
tugs dry leaves into the nest, does her duty.
While I—I'm afraid.
Even so, I desire nothing if not to stare
at the mysteries that take me back.
Conferences, schools, are so awful,
so full of stale coffee and sugar
that thought wanders:
God and his works are basic,
     male and female
     seven primary colors
     three realms
and one sole commandment: Love one another.
I was terrified of marrying a man
not from the Railroad;
I wanted household goods made of iron
so they would last forever.
I figured it like this:
if the bed was made of iron and the pots and pans,
God would take care of the rest:
clouds, dreams, memory.
Besides, I was not going to die, and I'm still not,
because I'm crazy and escape like the four-o'clocks.
At every graveside I cry with one eye only.
With the other I irrigate the strip of dirt
where bleeding hearts, everlastings and immortelles
are born to endure insects,
cycle after cycle of sun and rain,
heat of candles, cold of forgetfulness.
Because life is made of iron
and never ends.

Mobiles

What a beautiful poem if I can write it.
There's no shortage of tormented things,
farm produce awaiting transport,
and everything necessary:
I must make dinner.
Or supposedly ethical:
someone knocking at the gate—
Aunt Alzi hurries to the side yard to turn the panties
crotchside down on the grass.
An orange tree beginning to sprout:
a precious wildness presenting thorns,
miniature leaves, flowers whose petals
cluster in beads of sweet-smelling gold.
They explain the world as young chickens do,
perfect down to the nails, a plumed, living,
invincible delicateness
no man ever made with his hands.
Startled in bed with his hands over his ears,
the young man was saying: I can't sleep; it's the music from
                    the bar,
that rooster of yours crowing at all the wrong times.
Not true. It's because of life he can't sleep,
because of the hum that life makes.
He wants to get married and can't,
his job is lousy,
his pancreas a lazy ingrate.
I'm married and suffer as much.
The day goes by, the night, I step out of the shade and say:
This is all I want—
to sit in the sun until my hide is wrinkled.
But the sun, too, will disappear behind the hill,
night comes and passes over me;
far from mirrors, I feed dreams
of fame and travel, extraordinary men
offering me necklaces, words

that can be eaten, they're so sweet,
so warm, so corporeal.
The trellis sags with flowers,
I sleep a drunken sleep,
judging the beauty of the world negligible,
craving something that neither dies nor withers,
is neither tall nor distant,
nor avoids meeting my hard, ravenous look.
Unmoving beauty:
the face of God, which will kill my hunger.

About the Author

Adélia Prado was born and has lived all her life in Divinópolis, Minas Gerais, Brazil, a landlocked state of rugged mountains, mines, and baroque churches. She says of herself, "I am a simple person, a common housewife, a practicing Catholic." Her family were laborers; she was the only one to see the ocean, to go to college, or to dream of writing a book. She was graduated from the University of Divinópolis, earning degrees in philosophy and religious education, and taught religious education in the public schools until 1979. Since 1983, she has been cultural liaison for her native city. She began publishing her poetry when she was forty, and since then she has published eight books of poems and poetic prose. A theatrical production of her work was a sensation in 1987 in Rio and later on tour in Brazil.

About the Translator

Ellen Watson discovered Adélia Prado's work in 1980 and began translating her poems immediately. She worked on the translations with Prado in 1985 with the assistance of an NEA Translation Fellowship and traveled on a reading tour with her in the United States in 1988. Her daughter is Prado's namesake. Watson was a finalist for the 1984 Lewis Galantière Literary Translation Prize for her translation of the novel *Zero* by Ignácio de Loyola Brandão. She has translated five other novels from Portuguese and also writes poetry. A member of the American Literary Translators Association, the Northeastern Association of Brazilianists, and the New England Council of Latin American Studies, she is a graduate of the University of Massachusetts (B.A. 1974, M.F.A. 1979). Her home is in Conway, Massachusetts.

About the Book

The Alphabet in the Park was composed on a Mergenthaler Linotron 202 in Goudy Old Style, a typeface designed by Frederic W. Goudy (1865–1947), a former Midwestern accountant who became probably the most prolific type designer in printing history. The book was typeset by Brevis Press of Bethany, Connecticut. The design is by Kachergis Book Design of Pittsboro, North Carolina.